COME AND SEE

Books by Fanny Howe

POETRY
  Eggs
  Poem from a Single Pallet
  Robeson Street
  The Vineyard
  Introduction to the World
  The Quietist
  The End
  O'Clock
  One Crossed Out
  Selected Poems
  Gone
  Tis of Thee
  On the Ground
  The Lyrics
  Come and See

FICTION
  Forty Whacks
  First Marriage
  Bronte Wilde
  Holy Smoke
  In the Middle of Nowhere
  The Deep North
  Famous Questions
  Saving History
  Nod
  Indivisible
  Economics
  Radical Love: Five Novels
  The Lives of a Spirit / Glasstown: Where Something Got Broken
  What Did I Do Wrong?

ESSAYS
  The Wedding Dress: Meditations on Word and Life
  The Winter Sun: Notes on a Vocation

Come and See

FANNY HOWE

Graywolf Press

This publication is made possible by funding provided in part by a grant from the Minnesota State Arts Board, through an appropriation by the Minnesota State Legislature, a grant from the National Endowment for the Arts, and private funders. Significant support has also been provided by Target; the McKnight Foundation; and other generous contributions from foundations, corporations, and individuals. To these organizations and individuals we offer our heartfelt thanks.

Published by Graywolf Press
250 Third Avenue North, Suite 600
Minneapolis, Minnesota 55401

www.graywolfpress.org

Published in the United States of America

ISBN 978-1-55597-586-9

2 4 6 8 9 7 5 3 1
First Graywolf Printing, 2011

Library of Congress Control Number: 2011923186

Cover design: Kapo Ng @ A-Men Project

Cover art: Dr. Suzann Victor, *Third World Extra Virgin Dreams 1997*, 6th Havana Biennial, Cuba.
　　Materials: Human blood, glass slides, Fresnel lens, bed, clips.
　　Caught in a limbo of sleepless dreaming, *Third World Extra Virgin Dreams 1997* features a ten-meter glass quilt "descending" from both sides of an "ascending" bed. Staged in the Cabania Fortress at the 6th Havana Biennial, each of its three thousand pairs of glass slides and Fresnel lens hold a drop of blood taken from the artist and Cuban donor, Victor Miguel. Its surrealistic grammar is accentuated by the skylight, an architectural "orifice" that alludes to the body's paradoxical performance of "desire" and "revulsion" and/or "escape" and "entrapment."

Contents

A tree-
high thought
strikes the light tone: there are
still songs to sing beyond
humankind.

—*Paul Celan (translated by John Felstiner)*

COME AND SEE

This Eye

I see a child
between a star and a boat.
It is a silhouette
and there is the child again,
now attached to the boat.
All black.
Look at the weather,
the futile wipers beating!
I see the child on dry land,
now with his granny.
Like the boy in a story
he sees fire in wood and words
in smoke and he is good, too good
to be far from anyone old.

The father and the son
are still in a boat out there
with spinnakers
curved like pillows
where they can rest
their heads. Spin-drift
turns into curlews
confused by the weather news.

The sky is a fish packed in ice.
There is a low sun
and stiff silver wands
on the horizon
and the rudder groans
as the father and the ghost pass on.

No sun on a grate
but a migraine headache
and angry rain on the pavement.
The boy wonders
why a famous tyrant
marched his men into a blizzard
and how the Russians burned Moscow
with one candle.
He only sees three choices:
join, kill or run away.
What would his grandmother say?
Blessed are you when people hate you
and denounce you
for choosing eternity.

I have humiliated myself
so I can participate in the city.
I have smothered my own cries
in order to survive.
I have tied myself down
to the number system
so I can disappear into the stream
of the economy.
Whenever an old woman
is seen going
into a dark forest with two children
you know they are escaping.
They are not dying. Why else
would they be so bright of eye?

These long white days
have gone by with no recording.
Therefore they are free.
But what about the injustices
viewed from the window?
Intuitive women have power
over others but don't know it.
A boy reads about war
in bed with his grandmother.
She keeps getting up to look out.
What she sees horrifies her.
That's why she pulls the curtains
to protect the love she can't see.

"Granny, why do you care
where you are buried?"

Because I've lived
in my imagination.

"Granny, why don't we leave?"

Look down onto the street
at the children
with their heads shaved
and their skin too white.

Do you want to leave
this house and join the war,
my dark-eyed child?

"No, grandmother."

Let's pull down the shade then.
Open the book and read.

Some children went ahead
to enter a familiar enclosure.
Stepped the space
and were permitted occupancy.
A quick tap into panic.
Home was a continual theme.

Actually orphans were useful
out of fear of the touch of their keepers.
The children took care of each other
wrapping the littlest in wallpaper
ripped from their squat.
Warmth was as short of supply as hope was not.

The shell has opened into an esplanade.
People pour out, half formed
and opinionated.
The pouring is part of a plot
that is only readable in reverse.

For hundreds of days women and kids
defended their city with curses.
Men carried onions to them
across a lake half a foot thick
to put vitamins in their blood.

Praying and blinding
you feel what is happening at these times.
A girl turns again and again to make sure
she can believe what she has seen.
Then, for the others and the mice, she digs for bread.

Correspondence

Now a second snow
is falling on the first.

In a land of troubles
every snowfall is the same.

Even the hard-packed balls
outside the cathedral

remind them of stones
in emergencies above.

―――――

Pollen is summer snow.
The poplar trees break their pods

and little green boats
sail over the city

dropping white silks
on the pavement.

Some say they're bad.
Some say they're pretty.

They whiten the stones
from Chernobyl to the Winter Palace.

The Grotto

Let's make believe we're lying
together on our backs.
The lumps in the floor are dirt and grass
and the blackbirds tickle us with their claws
until we chirp and laugh.

This is fearlessness.

The sky wears no bells, no paper hats
but shawls crawl up the mountain rocks
piece by piece, and even under
night's weight
we still are not afraid.

The shawls are dragging themselves across the slate
that soon will cover our feet.
Black lace, black wool on the reeks.

I am now upstairs and you are down
in a white-washed cottage
packed in salt and wind.
The rooster's crow is not against the law.

Pretend we stamp the sand onto the floor,
then sweep away the crumbs and ticks.
Seagulls dock on the windowsills
and we spread the moon on a tablecloth.

You sip cold water from a silver glass.
I climb back upstairs with a hot water bag.
Tomorrow I get everything we need.
I mean today. I did.

Following Wang Bing

The ring road bends
for the Western Line.
Tracks break the ride
to a little town
like no other and gone.

Always coal-burning
smells, bitter
at the railroad depot.
Yellow snow
puffs on a bulb.

Here the workers
eat steamed dumplings
out of a tin.
So hungry they don't feel
the heat on their tongues.

Hands like teeth.
They share their stories
and their portions.
Workers did this
right through the programs.

The great programs
have ended.
One worker continues
to march with a torch
along the tracks

and frozen banks
scrutinizing the future.

He sings tenor.
In the end they only care
about each other.

The Rachmaninoff Hotel

The streets were full of the thundering young
who stamped their heels
to make us move along
as if we were the starved gone
who couldn't climb down
a long ramp underground or up the stairs to bed.
Inside my wood-perfumed room
I clung to a velveteen spread
as if splayed sideways in space but holding on.
What was our generation's definition
of the way to live? Something about action,
ideology, authority.
We wanted to kill those who are now us. Grown-ups!

Now I Have Seen Everything

The canal pipes smoked from the riverboats decorated in
    flowers and greens.
It was London 1910. A chill frosted the canal.
My play *I'll Quit If* took place that same season and my film
    of the play,
a hundred years later, was simply a ritual reenactment of the
    original.

At the end of Act One horrible people gathered
in an arboretum saluting a Nazi-to-be.
Thin-lipped men were dumped from limos onto the
    pavement,
crinolines and ankles flew after them.

When bus 98 passed containing one wounded and accusing
    face at the window
it was only a video of a sky-mind, a partial apparition,
He called to me to become a femme fatale who lives only
    for love
but it was not the call I was waiting for.

———

I want to know what happened to that cosmologist who
    kissed me
against a wall in public. He probably left the planet
with the watery eyes of a seer and still-soft lips.
In the old days scientists like him were cellists and chefs.

He followed me into my sitting room as I dozed. Each time
    I was blind and leaden,
unable to draw him close or even lift my hand.
Vivien Leigh went right up to Olivier on screen and inhaled
the aura around his collar instead of kissing his mouth.

————

You progress only by knowing you were wrong
and forgetting the context.
Like Franz Bieberkopf in the epilogue of *Berlin
    Alexanderplatz*
my heroine was humbled by every mistake.

I was too attached to innocence, according to the monstrous
    critic Reinart
whose brain was all he had.
When I say I, I mean Bieberkopf.
The pathetic ex-con was just as stupid as I am.

Two Aryan angels in brassy clothes
slid around candles in the street, it was decades before the
    film was made.
A platinum sky, a clear evening,
when the scientist whispered as if he were speaking into the
    ear of heaven.

My arms would not reach up to draw him down.
He was so cold, his wrist might have belonged to a priest
identifiable only to God and the idea of purity.
But his eyes in the microscope changed my future.

————

If he had the surrealist face of a French poet, I didn't know it.
Only that he wanted to skip the twentieth century
    completely.
He had a vision of it dropping into oblivion.
I reached up just as the curtain went down. I was very old
    by then.

He bent over me with the sadness of a specter.
We stayed like that with a floor-length window open onto
    the hangar
in an a-historical space. You can only confess once.
After that, there is very little to say about anything, especially
    a lost chance.

On the Wall

A map of heaven
shows clouds
for each soul
being prayed for.
The map appears
at certain hours
when the lace
cuts snowflakes
out of a hard wall.
Or when a car drives by.
And casts a square
yellow brick.

———

My bed is rising
but will never fly.
Immovable beads
of crystal
freeze my arms.
You have to understand
it was a wall-film I made.
A lady in waiting.
A fifteenth-century castle
and labyrinth.
Herself kept alive
by the tick of nail-clippers
behind her head.

Anniversary

Every February 27
someone would come and say,
Tomorrow Daddy will die.
There would be a corpse
still in action, a uniform, a badge.
The kazachok he learned
from the Russians
would be pounding on the floor.
The bed would be single.
He would be as noble as Thomas More.
Not smoking anymore.
But he would still have a tremor.
Yes, tomorrow he died.
I will now be able to bear anything.
I would have to, wouldn't I?

Written on Steps in Winter

I don't blame the children for anything.
Their century is like a director who prefers his script to
   his actors.
A robot who has false sex and no breasts.
The son is nervous and why not.
He spent his childhood on his mother's bed watching
   pornography and murder.

Some battered women go down
on their knees and faces, and kiss the glass
that covers the Blessed Mother. They'll only tell Her about
   the beatings they took.

Like most of them I was just one more person who had no
   skills or money.
My education was self-inflicted. This was an advantage.
The one-eyed woman is queen among the blind.
There is one who stands for hours
under a portrait of Bernadette of Lourdes.

She is an idiot savant and a saint. Thin as a book and long-
   skirted, her hands droop
at her sides. Bernadette looks flush by comparison, warm
   from the country air
and flashing her eyes at the sky.
Where this poor urban woman stands is in a dark cathedral
this hour and minute near the Gulf of Finland.

But what good is God to her
if all her work was only for the factory?

The multiplication of material? Her days are passed at a
    printing press
in a daze, fingers crippled and inked
shoving the content through the fire and holes.

What good was nationalism to her ancestors
endlessly at war with themselves and each other?
They cried out for 20,000 nights
to see a tyrant take shape
at the end of the bed and explain why it was all worth the pain.

Nothing happened. No one came. I was one of the lucky ones.
privileged to live a few decades in peace,
if without stature or particular beauty or grace or fame, just
    watching
and taking notes at the company gates.
I had healthy children and they did too. So what's the
    complaint?

For one thing my psychic didn't tell me I was a poet.
Now I can't be sure if I wrote
or am I the one walking up and up and up
the same stone steps. I can't rescue what never happened
though I came here to do so.

On my birthday the Germans aligned their warships alongside
    Russia.
This act led directly to the tragedy of Klimov and Larisa.
Just come and see their films about the Siege and Hitler.
Some have heard of their genius.

As a cultivated species who came out of the Enlightenment
to inflict pain on each other, you have to ask:
What good are humans to this poor earth?

It's the same question. What good is God to those crying out
    for help?
Are they crazy? Why can't they see that their work was for
    nothing
but money that went to the boss?
Why is it only the people in distress who keep calling for
    divine intervention?

What good was a voice to them when they shouted up
    for rain?
What good is eternal silence?
The curved sky with its percolating fires?
Why not rush through it, screaming, since you are here for
    such a short time,
just a spasm of cosmic information only half-discovered?

Where did the people get the idea of justice in the first place
if not from the losers, the wheat-carriers and the wounded
    who could not believe
in an earth without heart? The ones who worked the earth
and lived from it through famine and drought—
wolfing down the bread of heaven at night.

Out of It

During re-education
you can't learn.
Fear of the fist
produces self-censorship.

Thought wavers.
You fear ideas.
The ferry lets out a yelp
and you jump.

Your hands are numb
and nonfunctional.
They cover your lips
unable to utter a syllable.

What have you learned?

The nurse in blue
loosens your wristwatch
to let the blood flow.
Up you jump and run

when an angry man
comes in. This is a house
of true learning.
You must, you must
avoid that fist!

The Witness

Behold the broken
Hearts, backs and parts
Of nature
Evolved to follow
A finite path.

Behold the gray rain
In a house of mirrors.
Oak leaves shining
On glass, two kisses
In one spot exactly.

Behold the scabs and cuts
Of city streets.
Crusts, stones, smoke.
As many people
As nails from a factory.

Behold the space
Between each star
Or a child under nine
Laying her hand
On another's face.

Behold the foundation
And the secret of it.
Close your eyes
And breathe.
When seized, don't speak.

Passage

What else is an empty mother
but a waist behind a sweater
knitted to fit her at fifty, sixty, more?
Adult tastes in the music of her time.
Central London standing behind her
and beyond, a barley field,
its green pods spilling open.
Two pilgrim roses and two Rosa Glaucas
and twenty more she knows by name.

———

You can never
persuade one person that another
is a liar. People prefer the liar.

Honestly, with full knowledge.

People prefer ruthless power
because then they feel safe and they are.
He seems so sure, he is so sure
he could be a mother.

———

Her granddaughter fumbled frantically
with the buckle on her red purse
at the threshold, her head bowed
ashamed to cry at their good-bye.

———

God grant me the eternity
to complete this path:

The same one four days later
whipped in Didcot wind

by the nuclear power plant.

The shops and lifts
in the Templars Square.

Sitting on a wall
outside a bank, waiting for a child.

Out There

Each bird is another bird
Each robin a robin
Each tree is another tree
Each maple a maple
Each hop is a hop in time
Each root is a fastener
Each bird becomes a bird

After each hop a multiplier

Tree of seed
Tree of location
One two three—
A bird leads us away.

———

There is a little trouble in my eye.

Hurt is the same for all
But manifests itself as rage in one
And giggles in another.

I cry because my tear is glass.

One is a green bird with a black eye
One is a yellow bird with a red eye
One is a black bird with a blue eye
One is a brown bird with a golden eye

If you press the chest, there will be a song
Each one different from the other.
This is related to color.

All but paloma as gray as the sky when the snow is against
her.

The Hut

Up the hill is a hut made of sound
where two windows rhyme
and the tiles stay on
because they are nailed to a dream.
The dreamer wonders: Can this be mine?

The floor is solid and straight
and is amber from sap.
The walls don't leak or let out heat
from gray embers in the grate.

This is the original home
at the heart of brutalist design.
No storm can slam its shape apart.
No thief can carry it off.
It dwells in ashen buildings where the present sleeps.

After Watching Klimov's *Agoniya*

The peasant crosses from the farm to a train
And enters a tunnel to the palace.
The future watches him coming
Like a child whose doll falls from her hands when the living
    approach.
Ultimately he will be autopsied by nihilists
Who act like God and photograph his corpse.
The state goes on with its grim task of arresting its critics.
"Find me a person, any person, and I will find a way to
    discredit him."
What was alcohol for a peasant was heroin for Stalin.

The photographs of Rasputin's face make me wish I could
    meet him and vomit.
They are like unwrapped gauzes imprinted with mummies.
His voracious gaze, his wild hair.
They poisoned his cake and wine and shot him and shot him
    twice.
But he wouldn't die so they tossed him
Through a hole in the frozen river.
When the police found him, his arms were raised to lift the ice.
People dropped buckets into that superhuman water and drank.
Without an element of atheism, no religion can be credible.

A black frost dapples his face and torso.
They pickled his lingam; it was so long, they wanted to
    watch it.
He started life as a poor agrarian boy who got in trouble with
    the authorities.
Then he had a vision and walked from Siberia to Mount Athos.
Now he represents a question. What makes one person
Unable to inhabit his own skin? Once there was metaphysical
    socialism.
Call it Christianity. Or Gnosticism? Images of munitions
And wolves were sewn into his vestments. Because he was
    uncultivated,
He was dangerous. A serf, a monk and a drunk haunting the
    royal family.

We have to face reality.
We are glad we were born in the west. There. We said it.
Shame of *embourgeoisement* covers us.
Shame on behalf of the women and children who defended
    their city
Digging trenches in snow, Tarkovsky's Ivan,
Who lived in rooms smelling of wood and urine. Garlic, salt
    and black bread for supper.
The fountains play at the western palace from eight to five p.m.
The spouts work on a system of gravity that God or someone
    invented.
This discovery will become important to missile
    development.

What went wrong when we were young?
We had friends who became enemies of the state with us.
Students who turned into deserters, then returned to
    capitalism.
All was forgiven. So what did we fail to do then?
Carry through! Reconstruction was the next ideology.
Proud-bellied white men from the west got the last laugh.
Since the invention of the laptop, disconnected figures flow
From discarded works, phrases are resurrected.
Isn't this blasphemy like showing a saint in ballet tights?

When these four words—*You look well fed*— are said
You are doomed by your revolutionary companions.
You have no right to complain, having chosen to seek
A piece of the pleasure.
Some moments in history last too long.
They could have been whims but they became plans.
Beauty is a despised agent for religion under these conditions.
I open my eyes and can't hear a word from the days of
    rebellion
But when I close them, I hear "continuing revolution."

The spoils of a lost war (all wars dry up into scabs)
Have turned libraries upside down and texts are turned
    into clips.
Every old misery holds interest.
Father got worried when I went to the far left
And called me self-indulgent. Mother laughed
When I became a Catholic. She didn't believe it. I left the
    blackened house
And walked in the dark, throwing ballast overboard
For the sake of a future of solitariness.
To the seeker all objects are lonely and dangerous.

Great films begin in chaos.
They are made in order to show the abyss emerging into laws.
Like Pope John Paul, certain directors only want the splendor
    of truth.
Turgenev wonders if it is possible that all the tears and
    prayers of people
Can be fruitless? No, he protests. The indifference of nature
Is a foretaste of eternity and its mercy.
On the steps of the Czech embassy in London there is a
    splash of bird shit.
I sit beside it reassembling the bits of sound for this poem.
Words know everything. That's why my fingers shake.

Nietzsche was a saint but he made a mistake. He believed
  in humanity.
Almost everything in that café is weaker than the air that
  surrounds it.
Glasses hang upside down drying, a mirror reflects the room
  like an artist
Who is blind to what she is making.
Certain Gnostics achieve ecstasy through random and
  frantic sex
But love aches its way through the interstices.
Sticks there like a dent in an inchworm's back.
You can't take it out because it is the thing itself.
Love is the green in green. Does this explain its pain?

Since love came over and knocked me down,
Then kicked me in the side and fled,
I have suffered from a prolonged perplexity.
God is the object of my wonder and the closest to me.
Especially near sleep. My sheets are like the wings of a
  guardian angel.
There is no other fabric so near to my feelings.
I haunt a dark cathedral, its single light coming from the
  gift shop,
And follow the priest's movements, for here is the truth:
  both worldly
And eternal, a heart of gold in the roaring vault.

Here a weeping Madonna is kissed all day while an old
    woman wipes away the stain
With a gray cloth. The mass is focused on the resurrection
Not the passion. In this place a grandmother is called white if
    she has healing powers.
Rasputin had the power in his hands.
Yet Akhmatova shared a train compartment with him and
    felt faint
Looking at his pale eyes. Each iris, in either eye, saw around
    the pupil.
I feel sick looking at the photos of his eyes, his penis, beard
    and blood.
Violent, skinhead, racist, nationalist, sexist, illiterate men
Would appreciate him for the wrong reason.

Rasputin played dog and crawled into the royal dining room.
You smell like a mushroom, he barked and called on Jesus
To bless the soldiers who refused to kill the workers.
He was like dry root in motion.
Women loved him and let him achieve ecstasy on top
    of them.
This was his Gnostic and Tantric obsession. He lived
    without hate.
He could stop a migraine with his hands and was seen
Praying in a forest for hours on end and by his bed alone.
If only he had never taken up wine.

Now the children climb over the rails around the station.
The siege of renovation raised them, blocks and forests razed
And built on. Cement units they can't afford to live in.
The kids have behaved like spawn born to be the end of
      the line,
Or not fully born. Porn-driven thugs, Mafiosi, right wing
      Christians.
Only hope can save them, or an invasion by Muslims
      or oceans.
Who are dubbed the New Stupids? The workers!
The revolutionists were long ago strung up and the old did
      not survive the cold.
You could write music on the waterlines around their flooded
      tenements.

The peasant mocked institutions that Ratzinger would prize.
It was the student uprising of '68 that turned him against
      the Left.
Nowadays in every bureaucracy, including the Vatican, there
      are two of everyone.
Two of each who look exactly alike. It is the softness in
      the chin
That undefines them. Each one is the half brother of a twin.
Likewise Communism is secular Christianity.
Either you fear or thank someone and stay anonymous.
One poet recreated a new language out of his nanny's
      fireside stories.
This way his childhood survived, the way dinosaurs
      became birds.

While painting takes time and gives headaches,
A digital camera doesn't blink and this produces a lack of
    analogies.
It is not an open eye but an impure certainty.
Empty frames stand waiting under the stairs.
They wait for a thought that carried Dante with it, a long and
    difficult thought
Full of stains and imperfect figures, suffering and acid rain.
Don't plan any parties for Lent, a man called up in Italian.
And in the dream the shutter kept opening and closing
Like an anemone. Every hour was the same as the one before.

The roads we did not choose began in a town where we
    were born.
Here a gun might go off,
There perhaps a broom would brush away the sticks of spring.
It was not your fault where you were dropped
Or where you took your first steps.
The red church down the lane, the red sail on the bay—
These had nothing to do with you when you first arrived
    on earth.
A peasant might prefer smoking weed to whacking at wheat
    all day.
How else would a vision find and know him?

In a remote fishing village and on its wet stone steps
The clink of the ropes and rings on the boats was the
    only sound.
Then footsteps. The sun broke through onto buses and houses.
High up, a man and a woman, both old and on their own
Crossed paths without looking. Then she noticed him and
    he her.
A hurried exchange of recollections followed and
    half-promises to meet someday.
And then he continued to mount the side of the hill to
    his house
While she went down to the highway.
Absolutely nothing happened except recognition that left
    an ache.

The sorrowing face of the Theotokos blessed their simplicity.

At the Heart of It

The dirt is spirit
The people both
Celtic and Baltic.
Potatoes and onions,
Bread and beets.
Mystical, musical,
Violent and sad.
Without a way
Either right or left,
East or west.
But tears, plenty
Of tears to drink
While they dig.

Oil and Water

I'm flat out in a bed-sit in Jericho
while an Irish ship is leaving international waters
and heading to Gaza.
My underground studio
is comfortable and clean but I'm on my own
with this poem and the world situation,
and the pigeons who warble.

It's still spring.
The leaves have the watery fullness of birth
in them and flap their shadows green.
Parks, bikes, and unusual heat
are all outside and upstairs
beyond an iron railing.

The Irish boat is called the *Rachel Corrie.*
It has eleven passengers on board
who are not conceptualist or corporate
with minds discolored by
depressive German philosophy;
they are activists.

I'm discolored by the recent past,
and one of those still scratching
for a living in this bed-sit in Jericho.
Alone with a poem while the fridge
chews its cords and hisses
and a single fly spins around the room.

Salt and pepper!
Salt and pepper!
I am a lover-er
of Irish butter!

Rhythms, company.
You are never alone
but make the space around enormous
and distant
when it's indistinguishable
from anything else
you can't escape.

Rachel Corrie! Rachel Corrie!
Come in for dinner now.
My bed-sit is warm and the bread
pushed into the toaster oven.
We can cower together
until the twentieth century
has sunk like Atlantis and the sun.
A sinkhole in Guatemala?
Oil pouring from a hole in the water?
Is this what the residue
of radioactivity looks like?

The Irish are sailing to Gaza!
In the gulf the brown pelicans squat like icons
of the twentieth century
on a shelf
sliding with oil and water.

And that's why the sea level is rising.
Soon one hundred years will be covered
over, the swells of that catastrophe
will vanish and oil-drills
will emerge in new forms, the world
guided by its own inventions
and too much brain for imagination.

If I were not ill in this basement flat in Jericho
I would, I swear, volunteer to be
sailing to Byzantium
with Rachel and Gaza's children
and my book
of ancient Irish poetry,
entering the second century.

Someplace

A star is just a smudge
on magnified glass.
I have never been
more disappointed.
Nietzsche takes a saunter
along the border
because it is warm enough
to step out at night.
Malevolent blobs
dance at his feet.
This is when we pause to speak
in sleep. Our eyes
follow the lights while we ponder
which is worse:
Nothing or something you don't recognize.

The Color

If yellow could whisper, it did, for fourteen days and the
    summer nights stayed white.
Yellow walls, yellowish faces, 119 types of white person.
    A glow or none
From people who walked as if in line for bread. They pushed
    each other,
They stamped their feet.

They believed they deserved to starve for what they
    hungered for.

Because they were betrayed by people just like themselves
They whited out the area around that story.
And worked together with the dictator to create a plot
That included stupidity and could be erased.

Now the walls are freshly painted yellow.
The paper has been steamed away and the stone surface
    recolored.

There is a plant on every windowsill.

A little girl is surprised the leaves are fresh since the glass is
    so greasy
And the curtains webbed.
But inside she might see a fire and a kettle
Steaming for tea, and yellow cakes set out for the Resistance.

The Shape

We walked past riverboats on green canals
Until we came to a promontory.
There we viewed both the city and the sea.
I was two but one, and this was déjà three.

First there was the backside of Harlem
And a family of friends and then
There was a plaza with four roads and trams.
We knew our way through

By climbing and bending to the west.
We stood side by side as if we were one.
Often there were others sitting around
Or moving, listening to our angst.

They never said much. One night we two
Traveled to Belle Isle to buy a child
With a pageboy and a shy smile.
Who was foreign in such an improvisation?

We were multiple illegals in these dreams.
Escaped from other populations
And unnumbered streets.
Nobody said good-bye at the end.

Were we preparing to die?

A Hymn

"When I fall into the abyss I go straight into it,
head down and heels up and I'm even pleased
I am falling in such a humiliating position,
and for me I find it beautiful.
And so in that very shame I suddenly begin a hymn."

—F. Dostoevsky

I traveled to the page where scripture meets fiction.
The paper slept but the night in me woke up.

Black letters were now alive
and collectible in a material crawl.

I could not decipher their intentions anymore.
To what end did their shapes come forth?

To seduce or speak truth?

While birds swept over the water
like pot-bellied angels

beautiful bells rang to assist the hoist.

Up they went to slake their thirst,
drinking from the mist

for the sound of bells seemed to free
as well as hold them.

Then down to scavenge the surf
and eat the innocent.

"I love God and the ferry too," wrote Kerouac.

Only that which exists can be spoken of.

I wonder, will our imagination
remain a temple burning with candles

against all odds?
Behind a nipple and a bone?

The simplest of glands laid in a circle
around skin and liquid

that stirs up imagery
winged and prismed, as if blood

were a wine inducing visions.

Some people cry when the characters die.

Then they kill themselves offstage, away from the pages
that they are turning in the night.

Some people sacrifice themselves on a whim
and regret it later on paper.

Now I see you in the window.
Are you in the book I was looking for?

The one who traveled back to the happy days

when she could jump on a moving bus
and swing in the open air

clutching a worn novel in her purse . . . ?
A curtain, a knife, adoring eyes?

I watched the children running
and turned to Alyosha for a blessing.

He was sunk in the morass
of rural life

I like to sit with him in the grass.

Then we see the same thing at the same time,
and are one mind.

We two masses, one a book, one a hand.

When Alyosha spoke to the boys at the end
I anticipated their next question and his answer

for they formed a single gesture
of kindness.

"Will we?" "We will."

It seemed evil to read about people
we would never meet.
We tested their fortitude as if in sleep.
They generally failed the challenge
being strangers in a strange brain.

They were baffled by the tools
handed to them and by the traffic's direction.
Frankly in a dream or story,
the goal is absolutely hidden
from the one to whom it matters.

Eons of lily-building
emerged in that one flower.
Eons, eons. Pins
and wool, thread and needle,
all material
made of itself and circumstance.

It was a terrible century:
consisting of blasted
oil refineries and stuck ducks,
fish with their lips sealed by plastic
and tar in the hair of cooks.
Filth had penetrated the vents.

Institutions moan from the bowels.
Balls of used cotton
from the hospital dumpster, redden.
Yawning on obsolescence
the computer wonders

who punched in such poor grammar.
First-padded virgins
graduate to this suffering drama
all by her-selves.
Who once were cells.

History is more than just another surmising
grandmother at a window

or a reminiscence twisted in the scrim of translation.

Some long-ago light is pulsating in a trout's heart
on a laboratory dish.

That light has entered all the holes,
no matter how small, because it is the light that wants to live.

Still waiting for you my sunshine
of justice and mercy.

If west is east of Moscow,
depending where you're going

then will you ever find me
coming from a northerly direction?

Are you even looking at the earth?
Remember the map is flat but everything else is not.

Is the newest child the oldest body in creation?

Does he carry more information than his mother?

Does her mother, his grandmother, do *I* seem redundant
by having arrived with less, though first?

Is that why I read at night with my lips compressed?

The fact is, I never knew if anyone felt me
the way Nijinsky knew how to feel.

Or Nastasya. Nothing could shock that woman
who had done so much wrong.

As if trained in a theater, multiple personalities
streamed from her tongue.

This made her an exemplar for our time.

She knew how others felt and became each one,
forgetting who she was before.

I remember her as a child.

Her skirt got tangled up
in a thorn bush when she watched the sky.

Shaking herself free,
she had to see the spiders, ants and dirt
around her skirt.

It was like peering into her own body
and she screamed in horror.

Later, consolation
would be extended by a man dark and handsome:

It came with his semen
(when she wanted hibernation.)

She didn't commit suicide this time, but ran
down Nevsky Prospect as it began to rain,

and paused to lift her umbrella.
For this moment

we were in our soul a child
rushing home to granny five floors up.

I dropped the book, wept and went to the movies.

It is here where I can forgive someone for his crime.

Poisoning babies for profit. Harry Lime.

I can actually forgive it when he is crawling in shit.

Otherwise we will stand on the Ferris wheel together forever.
stuck in the fog and iron.

I just a witness to his ironic story

He will be a mix between Paul Celan and Oscar Levant
when we are at our happiest
and no forgiveness is asked.

Neurotic, pale, and drawn to the canals,
we will lean over the embankment like sister and brother

who are tempted to be actors.

It is here that his shoes and cat
will converge in the dark. Like fish in a secular city

flipping through sewers for a flash of Christ.

The Interpreter

There are two hundred acres
of this twisted lake.

A child turned some knights
into enchanted mermen
at the bottom of the water
where their arms now swing
in the weeds.

Some day this country will be free
of knaves.
(Oppressed people
always believe these things.)

Now there is ice on every twig
and splinter of bark.
Where one sees Narnia,

the other sees a nuclear winter.

The potential is beyond history
where we'd all like to be.

Oh and then there's revolution
and hallucinogen

until someone comes from outer space
or nature goes insane.

If all the elements are logical
but one that will never fit in
and stays apart from the whole system
without a name or a slot,
what will it be?

It will be a question:

"Is he coming today?"
"No. Go back to sleep."

After Seeing *The Ascent* by Larisa Shepitko

A man went into a fortified country.
It was snowing, his back was broad.
He wore a round fur cap
and seemed partially blind.

Only such a man would dare to enter
a transnational cemetery
where the markers are gone.
Old snow stuck to them.

I was yards away from the man
and the gate, but I could see his face
with my zoom lens.
His coat was the gray of a rat.

The two-state solution had failed.
Or was it one. I can't recall.
Only that peace was impossible
unless the man in the cap

could absorb all the
revenge and sorrow
into himself and carry them out
of the fortified land.

What is peace, you might ask,
if not freezing dysfunction
in one position
for a few more years.

His face was screwed up
from the cold, his eyes were large
but far away.
He had lived in the heart

of the twentieth century
His breath was salty with pity.
He went in without a plan
to exchange grudges or bodies.

Instead he opened his arms wide.
and breathed deep,
gathering the shrieks
and shouts into his lungs.

Of course it hurt the way thorns
rip blood from thin skin.
But the people were heedless
and clawed to get in.

This was a secular first:
a post-Marxist, self-made scapegoat
whom nobody noticed.
They were ruled from the grave.

Mothers, children, old people,
whirled as if blown
by a north wind, and only weighed
as much as their hearts.

No, it was their agony.
The foreign man took them
in his arms and staggered
out of the fort again.

Then he swayed in the snow,
for a second, and fell
recalling a single perfection
which was enough for him.

On his back, looking up,
weighed down by the stuff
he had carried out,
he remembered Larisa and her film.

It was called *The Ascent.*
And showed her to be a saint.
Then the man let himself forget
everything human and get drunk.

He was glad to escape that land,
to drop the miserable dung
that didn't belong to him,
like any job that just has to be done.

Remembrance

I had three learned friends,
None of them had power.
or even a desire for it.
A grotto and conversation
made them happy enough.

The grotto might be a hellhole,
where all three had the ability
to care for someone else
whom they chose
because they knew how to loathe.

For each God was a word
for whatever falls
outside knowledge, language and light.
So they didn't study for a promotion
but watched the horizon.

Inescapable

A stone abutment
over a teashop.

The boxwood pruned
and sweetish.

A cat lapping
at raindrops on a leaf.

———

The monk's eyes look up
from his grave.
Fresh cut freesia on it.
A yellow jug of milk.

A beam of light slams
on the granite.

Pages of stone
now contain information.

Seen

A real bungalow
is made of stone
and snow white mud
on the inner walls,
a large grate
and a slate floor
and a picture of itself.

Every cupboard is old,
every glass and cup
wiped clean.
The wind cannot get in
so the flies are free
to buzz against the glass.

Outside, blue twine
is tied to a telephone pole
and a gate
to keep the brown cows
in their field.

Fuchsia hedges, clover
in full juice:
purple clover, purple heather.

There's a silver line
on the sea between
green sheer islands:

Now the sound of the wind
playing a foghorn
enters forgotten.

On the Beach

White night.
White breakers.
North June and silver.
White sky, white sheets.
Sick at Omaha Beach.

Green climbs the crest.
Birds on clinical alert.
Little white boats sited
from the ferry crossing.
Iceland time zone.

Lenin long gone, Vichy,
Eisenhower, cows like sows
in Normandy by the highway.
Atlantic wash-ups, white
as an awning of ice.

But a feverish drizzle
softens the salt black.
A mothering misery
semi-sleeps in fog
and roses pale.

Old Blighty's children built
pontoons in the sand,
landing in the white light
of a dawn interrupted
by a slash of black.

So much to disconnect.
Their cries for home
half-ecstatic at being lost
will be broken into shots
of blood and surrealist poets.

Heroin taken, injuries
crippling, heroics abandoned,
until sex and its replicating angles
bring us new children
and their acts of resistance.

What Did You See?

for Peter S.

I saw the shrouds of prisoners
like baptismal gowns
buried outside the cemetery.

On the canvas frills exhaled
singed wool and cardboard.

The angels arrived as lace.

Took notes, then stuck. Awful residue
from a small cut.

———

The veil has been ripped from the skin
where it was burned in.

The skin is the veil, the baby-material,
imprinted on, as if
one dropped the handkerchief
and it was one's own.

The cuff is frightening.
Stuffed onto oil.
Water-stains might fence its ghost in.

———

"The barbed-wire complex"
I understand.
Winged and flattened
at the same time, poor things!

Some leftover specters of blood.

Remember Blake's figures like columns
with heads

looking around for God?
When things are not as random
as they seem.

———————

The article of clothing
is only half there, it's not full,
but when it falls forward, it is.

Terrible emptiness of the spread
neckline and little sleeve.
Half-cooked squares.

Was this religious fire
and is this where it passed?

Maybe they are floating on water
of paint, pool-sized,
blue and ridged like foam.

You would have to fly
to see them flat as a map.

The rib and hem. Rained on
for eons. Noah's children's
floating forms.

───────

Angels die?
It's a frightening-miracle
because here they are.
The Upper God

has let them drop
like centuries into space.

And I recognize them!

Flying Carpets

The earth is a flying carpet
if you lie down and follow
the clouds. Where will it go
with you upon it?
And shelters stuck below.

Cars, caves, hotels and shacks
for the old who (if they could)
would become mystics
and monastics, dignified by
disciplined hours of reminiscing.

Each would have his and her
own carpet, an ever-filling bottle
of water, one of spirits,
a lump of bread a day
and sweet jelly.

Each would loll and float
accepting the situation.
Heavenly contusions from the roll
through the halls
of kismet on a carpet cut to painfully fit.

Aladdin closed his eyes
beside me on the shag.
It was flight twelve at night
returning to the peripheral estuaries.

The heavens were never a hidden metaphysics
but the stars in their circuits
and our eyes until blinded by sunset:
an Ayurvedic cure.

Many choose to get high
rather than struggle
with wickedness. Scatter rugs
to our mother's chair
lead us like bridges to Islam
built from mist and sun.

Babies crawl over them
as if on a carpet of flowers
that will float one safely seated upon it.
Aladdin bravely and scarily
dares to sleep in space
as if on a wall.

But would you call it peace
in a busy white desert
with feasting creatures
going at each other?
Would you smile and call it natural?

Would you call God good
if it didn't hold the crying baby?
Or lead the dromedary home?
Then to whom can you holler
at the sound of children in pain?

Only to the next one over
on a carpet under the sky.
She is expecting a baby in August.
Wants a girl.
But they are so poor
and good-natured, they will probably inherit the earth
and not the flat in East London.

The prayer rug floats by
like a six-foot plot
littered with pins and needles
from a tailor's labors.

God is not God
sitting with Aladdin
in the early morning,
our eyes closed up.
God is aeronautics and orange.

We fold up to make a nest.
Behind our eyelids
Tibetans move freely
in the darkness without dreams.

I am afraid to shut my eyes for too long
for fear that the evil one
will jump me from behind.

Then the air seems to pour into a form.
Clamps down my arms.
Grasps and blinds me.
Little people from everywhere
fly in laughing and take over
the township I carry around.

If I can unlock my arms and see
I can join them in a parade
in the Square. For there they are:
deep down, woven into the carpet
with the tailor's blood-spots
and society.

No flying carpet was invisible.
Always a tapestry of curlicues
green, maroon, or big and blue
under your feet on some floor.

Aladdin flew by fresh air
like those of us at a picnic
in Holland Park, dotting the grass
speaking of Afghanistan
and the Taliban to the soft pop
from a tennis cork.

Mangoes were chopped
near the concrete post-bombed
buildings in lumpen-brat
compositions
prophetic of Baghdad's ruins
and the exploding refineries
that the Bushes added to the atmosphere.

The new creation will be lifted
above the crowd like Jesus
who was circumcised from earth,
not a remnant left.
What is a prophet but one
who can see as if from the sky

the yellow musk of winter clouds
trailing the rugs that lie across the fens.
Whiteouts of the work done
on past nests displayed
as little baskets in trees.
The whole event is one event
and a circle.

The shadows of these carpets
will be colorless
over the unconscious city
and its citizens
who won't open the gates
to boys like them.

But Swami said:

"Time is not straight!
A child's view
is the true one.
Do feed the doll fruit
and cereal. She
in the husky blue dress
and sparkles
will be lifted up."

A Vision

Little boy
dressed in blue
like a mountain-bend:
when we walk today
hold my left hand
for the other one is on my right.

Boys, boys, don't fight.

Some floors shine like walnuts, red,
some are brick but porphyry,
the square kind.

One tile has a six-inch map
(from a crack on it)
for you to follow anywhere you want.

The white light on the windowpane.
That square blur on the floor.

Are sallow inconsequential signs
of something to come:

a bigger gold and tangible.

Its primary goal
is for Utopia.
This includes
a cemetery for all.

No distinction
between ashes.
A village rich
in the tradition

of altruism
as something striven
for, over centuries
of rape and war.

———

Rome is as close
to a walnut
as a book is
to a tree.

Come and See

The image of an iron bed rising upwards with strands of broken glass descending, each shard containing a tiny drop of blood, and overhead a dome that has the markings of an inverted Earth, shown at the Cabania Fortress in Havana, 1997, and called *Third World Extra Virgin Dreams* . . . makes an observer wonder: did this really happen, or was it constructed?
Why does it seem as if this room existed in real time as the result of historical events?

The photograph has "that look" that we recognize as nearly our own. *Didn't I sleep there?* It is something we don't dare ask while we pass it around to strangers.

To me, the "extra virgin dreams" of the title may elude to the surreality of an event reconfigured only in a dream without a sleeper . . . the sleeper being the artist who also shares her blood with the living, or the one departed from the bed.
The bed might be a bed made out of nails heading for the stars.

The sleeper-artist is the keeper of this image and now part of a tradition digging at the litter of the twentieth century and redeeming it in the base materials of suffering.
The bed could be the bed of an orphan, a lonely visionary, or a ward of the State.
You don't want to say too much about such an image. It arrives at a level equivalent to the dreamer's and will not be relieved of its mystery through words.

A picture that lifts up a piece of history and reveals its nonchalant mission, is sacred.

What do I mean when I say "sacred?" I have to wonder, since the most sacred places in modern times are those where massacres and extreme injustice occurred.

How to come to terms with this paradox is, for me, the struggle of every kind of thinking, feeling person—artist or butcher.

Sacredness is a term that is limited to a few public places on earth, to a few events, rituals and objects. Each of these is invested with a power that exceeds its limits.

Sacredness indicates a second face under the given.

If everything is sacred, then the word would be unnecessary. So, as long as the word is necessary, its meaning is particular and strong.

A few months ago I was surprised by the discovery of a three-page document I hadn't seen before when I was emptying out boxes of papers and letters in my attic. It was written by the novelist and teacher Ilona Karmel. She had typed it herself and had made a few corrections. So why didn't I recognize it? It seemed like a short speech she might have been asked to present before reading aloud from her novel.

To me the discovery was similar to the "message in the bottle" that Paul Celan used to describe his poetry.

The message was both casual and deeply thought and its purpose was to explain why she had been compelled to write her masterpiece, *An Estate of Memory*.

My purpose, writing this now, is to share this thing of value from the twentieth century and in particular from the war that has haunted our world, from painting to film to poetry, as a collective nightmare. The experience of that time belonged to Ilona's generation, though the residue of the experience has glowed in the structures of literature and philosophy and other arts, like pieces of shrapnel in a patient's brain.

———

Like Dostoevsky, Ilona Karmel pursued truth (without quotes) through a relentless and unfavorable account of human behavior, interrupted fleetingly by something wonderful and unexpected.

She wrote: "I began my novel with only one assumption; that man lives in constant tension between contradictory forces within himself, above all what I would call 'the everyday and the Sabbath'—his awareness of himself as he is, and his longing for what he wants to become."

Karmel and Dostoevsky had experienced the worst in human behavior, mostly inside prisons, and were unable to forget it. Both used the common word "freedom" for the moment when an unforeseen act of self-abandonment occurs. This moment of freedom releases one from the everyday and the inevitable, and sometimes has the reckless look of suicide.

For both of them—if they failed to find a trace of that freedom in their long labors at writing and remembering—life would continue as a dazzling after-effect of hell, a mirage of trauma, like the lightning-fast Shoah in Hiroshima.

———

In order to trace the path of an unselfish act through plot and character one would have to account for every troubled step around real rooms, barracks, cells, and streets. It would involve making this exceptional act inevitable in relation to one person's character in the midst of causes and contingencies.

The everyday life of people in prison or war is not at all ordinary, and it is not science fiction. Its extreme abjectness and drudgery encourage both false claims and self-censorship. To make any gesture that transcends such a situation would be incredible.

But for such writers as these, "transcendence" was not part of the equation. Paradoxically, each wanted to take the mystery out of self-sacrifice and prove its place in human personality, while at the same time revealing it to be an unpremeditated gesture, or one act that lacks the logic of will.

———————

At the conclusion of her essay, Karmel wrote:

"Somehow halfway through the book I realized that my characters—though none of [Janusz] Korczak's stature—were following in his footsteps. I tried to describe those steps as exactly as I could. . . . To describe this is all the book attempts to do; not to accuse or complain (the time for this has passed), nor to propound a thesis, just to describe the changes which, from the shabby origins of our love, can lead to this act and this death."

Korczak was the teacher and writer who founded an orphanage during the war in the Warsaw ghetto, and died voluntarily (the SS offered him his freedom) in Treblinka with the children.

It was the unaccountable quality of a life like his that made her weave her way through the thicket of plot in search of an explanation for it. She had witnessed, in the camps, an act of self-sacrifice on the part of a young girl that she could not forget. (A pretty blond teen who was considered superficial, put herself, spontaneously and voluntarily, in place of someone else on the gallows.) And she saw smaller acts of radical kindness, none of them determined by convention but by an extreme lucidity.

Her fiction is a documentation of days as she experienced them in a particular period.
As if being constructed as a record for later historians, it's painstaking in its accumulated detail. Shoes, foods, jewels, barracks, beds, snow, and faces. The characters are neither good nor evil but described inside folds of necessity. It would have to be this way when nothing was sacred.

The story involves a struggle to recognize the world as it is given when it is given at its worst. How do people stay sane when others, just like themselves, behave in unrecognizable ways?

———

I know that it took her ten years to write the novel. She was in Germany with her husband then, and working in an orphanage. She made a vow. She would write down what had happened during the war with the sole desire to salvage meaning from the facts, to rescue the integrity of the people who had struggled with their shortcomings when corralled into slavery and had, in a few cases, changed for the better. She loathed sentimentality, especially about people who endured prison camps during the war.

To redeem them from the smear of pathos by making their difficult personalities real again, and then to see what would happen, was part of her goal. In other words, to see what a human being is in relation to ethics, others.
She stripped her characters, one by one, of passively accepted values, and tested them in a world where anything was possible, even killing children.

Her purpose was more than a demand that we remember what happened.
It was a demand that we rescue meaning (what is just possible, about to be born) . . . to rescue human beings from self-loathing by reminding them of acts of charity.

She wrote, in her essay: "Terrified and alone one turns to others, not out of love, just out of the desperate and self-centered need for comfort. Those are the shabby beginnings of our love. Yet gradually a transformation occurs. He who knows how to grant comfort becomes the guarantor of hope, the keeper of one's image of oneself. . . . No ideals of self-sacrifice or courage are now at work. Just the inner necessity to defend what has become too precious to be destroyed."

And this explains why she called the essay "Keepers of the Image."
Those who are keepers of images are people selected to hold a precious object safe. They are entrusted with the work of

protecting, say, the Emerald Buddha, the Torah, or the Virgin of Guadalupe from the onslaught of wars and plunders.

They have taken a vow to do so because of the singular nature of the image itself. The image is a representation of a secret self, the being one longs to be, the self one never was in history, but remembers. The keeper's vow sweeps aside everyday life for the sake of a distant achievement. Everyday life is both the cover for the image, and the vehicle for the vow.

Often this involves a vision of something as yet uncreated.
The vow to enter the future might be addressed to a distant point outside of oneself, but its source remains tangled in the interior, like the beginning of a little cry. The cry is aimed into an infinity of air, or an ear of infinite depth, expecting to be heard somewhere by a You whom we do not know, a kind of eternal estate of memory.

The vow to protect an image is a way of transcending the days you pass through by holding something that is not yet realized in human form, holding it against you, in secret.

You might vow to stay true to someone until the end of your life. You might vow to spend your life working on a peace agreement. To see a child grow up. Or to finish a piece of work. You cannot vow to see something happen that you wish would happen, however. You can only vow to labor for that something. (In a sense, this is what makes revenge dependent on lies and dishonesty.)

When a person becomes the keeper of an image, it requires a vow that is strange. This is because the significance of the image is only revealed in the act of preserving it, and the vow to be the one who sustains that significance must continually endow it with attention to the exclusion of real life, the everyday passing.

For Karmel, the vow to write the record of that time, to take as long as was needed to complete the documenting, ensured her status as the keeper of an image.

In the same cardboard box, under more papers, I found handwritten notes that Karmel had made, perhaps for a class, on passages from Proust, Henry James, and Franz Rosenzweig. And then there were two pages of random observations of the sort that are found in notebooks, but in this case they were on loose sheets. They struck me as many such writings do, as having a power in their very roughness and haste.

Spontaneous writing suggests, if nothing else, a poetic way— that is, a way that includes a non-performative and non-egoistic reportage. Like the notes of Simone Weil written during her three weeks in a transit camp in Casablanca, unedited and unsolicited, these cuttings from Karmel's thoughts help us see that she looked for meaning in every spare moment, how swiftly it comes and goes.

The very fact that she wrote poetry in Buchenwald suggests that poetry itself is a part of the mind reserved for resistance to force. Poetry doesn't just help someone survive, it is a survivor itself: fluid, protean, as it passes through walls, and brings a particular beat to a way of thinking and being.

———

In other words poetry is not just a set of enjambed lines on a page. It is not just poetry.

Ideally poetry reveals the face of justice through syntax, balance, image. That is, the harmony strung between two disparate images.
It doesn't give more to one than to another.
It's visible in all things that are unfolding and disappearing.
It offers a trace of freedom. And so it's the opposite of oppressive, opinionated, controlling or controlled.
The word "image" is central.

In our time now, the proliferation of images showing the distance between the earth seen from miles above and the globe, its ground stained by rubbish—these images inspire ghastly fear, not just awe, because there is no particular harmony between the two. Are these the few pure remnants of the work of the twentieth century? Works of technology rather than imagination?
And another question—can we recognize ourselves?—stays with us, just as warm arms and kindness remain basic to our existence.

In a constructed installation like *Third World Extra Virgin Dreams*, we recognize a loneliness that is sacred to survival. The image, preserved, reminds us that there are still ways to exceed the boundaries of the given, ways that still depend on the laws of nature.

How can we meditate on the new visions of time and space without remembering that physics produced the bombs over Japan and now, having accomplished that, will take us to another drama, or trauma? This is where we stand, face to the sky, waiting for the next readjustment to our self-image. Materialized and identified, but instantly gone from past to past to past.

A leap out of one's seemingly determined fate (an act of charity) can come from any number of experiences as the novel, *An Estate of Memory*, labored to prove, and this message is offered to the twenty-first century as something to be treasured. More than ever, now: to believe there is something that is not simply a norm.

In a sense, when this epiphany takes place, it is a miracle. A miracle is an event that changes the meaning of things. It is like a thought that floats free of the surrounding systems and conventions, and enters, uninvited, a sentence, a stanza, a conversation, a lab result, and sends it on another path.

A miracle can be the appearance of another person rising out of an emptiness that we are beginning to accept as permanent. As Paul Celan wrote, it is "**A rumbling**: it is / Truth itself / walked among / men, /amidst the / metaphor squall."

Acknowledgments

These poems were written during a period when I was very lucky. I received a Guggenheim Fellowship, went to the Bellagio Foundation in Italy, traveled around Ireland, worked in St. Petersburg in Russia, received the Ruth Lilly Award from the Poetry Foundation, spent time in England and at Civitella Ranieri in Umbria, and won an award from the American Academy of Arts and Letters. Thanks to all of these, I was able to increase the tempo of my itinerant way of life and enter the world as I found it, without depending on a paycheck.

What I saw was what I became: that is, one of the people aging in various stages of usefulness, unbelief and loneliness, a relic of the twentieth century and its ceaseless wars, failures and technological advances, and a lover of films that helped me understand and survive these conditions. Two made by Elem Klimov and Larisa Shepitko seemed to grasp the essence of our cultural ambivalence especially well, but there were many others. Movies generally gave me a meditative and focal point for my sense of things, as did the liturgy at the cathedral Kazanskaya and the offices at Glenstal Abbey and music. I saw the paintings of Peter Sacks in an upstairs gallery in New York and tried to answer the question: What did you see?

My gratitude to organizations that grant free time to people like me is boundless, and my indebtedness to editors of magazines and books who still publish poetry is too. Some of the poems published in this book have appeared in these publications: *Black Renaissance Noire, Granta, Life as We Show It: Writing on Film, Maggie,* the *Nation, Poetry, St. Petersburg Review,* and *Salzburg Review.*

The epigraph by Paul Celan is from *Selected Poems and Prose of Paul Celan,* translated by John Felstiner, and published by W. W. Norton, 2001.

Fanny Howe is the author of more than twenty books of poetry and prose, including most recently *The Lyrics* and *The Winter Sun: Notes on a Vocation.* She received the 2009 Ruth Lilly Poetry Prize from the Poetry Foundation for lifetime achievement, and she has won the Lenore Marshall Poetry Prize and the Gold Medal for Poetry from the Commonwealth Club of California. She lives in New England.

Come and See has been typeset using Trump Mediaeval, a typeface designed by Georg Trump and first issued in 1954 by the Weber Foundry, Stuttgart, Germany. Book design by Ann Sudmeier. Composition by BookMobile Design and Publishing Services, Minneapolis, Minnesota. Manufactured by Versa Press on acid-free 30 percent postconsumer wastepaper.